Mastering Situational Leadership

Lead with Confidence and Maximize Employee Potential

By

Liam Davis

Author Bio

Liam Davis, author of this guide and an expert in leadership dynamics, brings a fortune of his understanding and experience through "Mastering Situational Leadership." Liam Davis holds an outstanding career record in different leadership positions, where he has refined his skills and expertise in dealing with challenging situations and developing the potential of his team. This insightful guide demonstrates his sensible approach, and in-depth understanding of situational leadership. Liam Davis's devotion to creating future leaders shows through his composition of this guide as he addresses how to lead with confidence and uncover your employee's full potential. "Mastering Situational Leadership" displays Liam Davis's passion for building effective leadership competencies for the current dynamic organizational environment.

Contents

Author Bio -3

Introduction -6

Chapter 1: Understanding Situational Leadership - - - - - - - -8

1.1 Explaining the Concept of Situational Leadership 9

1.2 The Role of Flexibility and Adaptability in
Leadership. 14

1.3 Why Situational Leadership is Crucial 22

1.4 The Significance of Situational Leadership Learning . .23

Chapter 2: Examining Four Main Leadership Styles - - - - -25

2.1 Telling (Style 1). 26

2.2 Selling (Style 2). 27

2.3 Participating (Style 3) 28

2.4 Delegating (Style 4) 29

2.5 Evaluating Your Default Leadership Style. 30

Chapter 3: Constructing Powerful Foundations - - - - - - - -36

3.1 Establish a Leadership Mindset. 37

3.2 Trust as the Foundation of Effective Leadership 40

3.3 Role of Effective Communication in Leadership:
Vital Skills and Strategies for Greater Productivity 42

3.4 Ways to Establish Leadership Credibility 45

Chapter 4: Navigating Difficulties and Resolving Conflicts in Leadership -49

4.1 Common Challenges in Leadership and
Suggestions to Overcome Them 50

4.2 Conflict Management Techniques in Leadership 53

4.3 How to Transform Obstacles into Opportunities 57

Chapter 5: Boosting Employee Ability - - - - - - - - - - - - - - - -60

5.1 Encouraging Empowerment with Situational
Leadership. 61

5.2 Promoting a Mindset of Growth 63

5.3 How to Provide Constructive Feedback to Your
Employees as a Leader 66

Chapter 6: Lead with Assurance and Confidence - - - - - - -68

6.1 Ways to Develop Leadership Confidence and
Overcome Self-Doubt 69

6.2 Mastering The Art of Resilience in Leadership 71

Conclusion -74

Introduction

The notion of situational leadership acts as a guiding compass in the domain of leadership, lighting the way to practical and flexible management. For a while, I have travelled across the complicated landscape of leadership and have observed deeply the hurdles and accomplishments that leaders encounter in the dynamic environment of the working place. I have understood, as a specialist in situational leadership, that influential leadership is not a standardized strategy but is a skill of adaptation to various events.

Visualize Emma, an experienced professional, pushed into a post of leadership supervising a crowded department in a burgeoning tech firm. Emma, enthusiastic and determined, at first accepted the new task with passion. But as soon as she grappled with overseeing a group with different personalities, work techniques, and aspirations, the truth of leadership intricacy became clear.

The journey of Emma acts as the context for the narrative of mastering situational leadership. Imagine her meeting closed project deadlines, every member of group answering distinctively to the pressure. As Emma seeks to comprehend her group's various abilities, weaknesses and inspirational triggers, the importance of situational leadership becomes obvious.

Emma's comprehension mirrors the hardships that leaders encounter in the working environments. In the atmosphere of diverse and vibrant staff, traditional leadership theories are not sufficient, requiring a more refined and adaptable strategy.

My own close observation of leadership dynamics and expertise as a leader generated my fascination to write down this essential guide.

In today's world, multiple leaders are unaware of the complexities of situational leadership. This book functions as a comprehensive guide, which not only demonstrates the concepts but also offers practical techniques to leaders in order to take charge with full confidence and unseal the full abilities of their teams.

I invite you to join me in this investigative study of situational leadership, where theoretical concepts encounter the realistic problems of the work environments. This book provides a road of discovery, where leadership encounters flexibility and adaptation and teams prosper under the direction of assured leaders. My goal is to equip leaders with all the necessary mechanisms needed to effortlessly adjust their leadership style in diverse circumstances, promoting outstanding success for themselves and for their teams.

Concurrently, let's untangle the coatings of situational leadership and authorize ourselves to oversee with effectiveness and knowledge.

Chapter 1: Understanding Situational Leadership

To be more thriving in the work environment, leaders can implement many styles of leadership. Situational leadership is among one of these styles, in which leader alters their type of leadership depending on the particular task or scenario.

In this chapter, we will examine the different aspects of situational leadership, starting from its definition to the importance of its learning. This chapter acts as a strong giving structure for an in-depth study of the principles of situational leadership. So let's get started.

1.1 Explaining the Concept of Situational Leadership

Situational leadership is a particular style of leadership in which the leader adjusts their overseeing style to complement the present atmosphere of work or requirements of a team/group. This leadership style is not completely based on the skills of the leader; instead, it is based on the capability of the leader to adapt to the needs of an organization or team to become a competent and more successful leader.

This style of leadership, which is also known as the " Model of Situational Leadership" or "Theory of Situational Leadership", was initiated by Ken Blanchard & Paul Hersey while developing the book Management of Organizational Behavior.

1. Styles of Leadership

According to Hersey and Blanchard, there are around 4 main styles of leadership, and based on the scenario, a situational leader may utilize one of these behavioral styles of leadership.

- **S1 (Telling):** The leader commands individuals what to accomplish and how to accomplish it in this particular leadership style.

- **S2 (Selling):** This style implicates improved interchange between leaders and their followers. In order to convince group participants to take part in the process, leaders "sell" their theories and message.

- **S3 (Participating):** In this strategy, the leader delivers fewer guidelines and permits group members to take an active position to come up with concepts and make judgments.

- **S4 (Delegating):** This approach represents the style of leadership that is uninvolved and hands-off. Members of the group make the majority of decisions and take the majority of accountability for what occurs.

Leaders employing the situational leadership style will utilize the style that is best fitted to a situation since no singular style is believed to be the finest for a leader. It totally depends upon the situation.

2. Levels of Maturity

The correct leadership style relies strongly on the level of maturity (i.e., the understanding and competence level) of the group or people.

Theory of Hersey and Blanchard specifies 4 different maturity levels, such as:

- **M1:** Members of group lacking the understanding, abilities and readiness to finish the assignment.

- **M2:** Members of group are keen and passionate, but don't have the ability to do so.

- **M3:** Members of group have the talents and ability to finish the task, but are not willing to commit.

- **M4:** Members of group are highly trained and inclined to finish the task.

3. Aligning Styles and Levels

Maturity levels and Leadership styles can be aligned. The model of Hersey and Blanchard presents that the following styles of leadership suit these levels of maturity the best:

- **(M1)** Low Maturity — (S1) Telling
- **(M2)** Medium Maturity — (S2) Selling
- **(M3)** Medium Maturity — (S3) Participating
- **(M4)** High Maturity — (S4) Delegating

4. How It Functions

At the start of the project, when members do not have the commitment or understanding to work individually, a better "telling" style might be required. The leader may like to take an additional delegating strategy once underlings become more skilled and acquainted.

Leadership with situational strategy also sidesteps the perils of the one-style strategy by realizing that there are a lot of manners to handle the problem and that leaders must be capable of evaluating a circumstance and the levels of maturity of underlings to decide what strategy will work best at the particular situation.

Consequently, situational approaches provide a more significant review of the active social circumstances and the multiple people functioning in diverse roles who will eventually help shape the final result.

5. Benefits of Situational Leadership

Many advantages are linked with situational leadership; these advantages serve both the organization or team and the leader. Some of the advantages of situational leadership include the following:

Leaders are free to utilize whichever style they think is appropriate in a given circumstance.

This leadership type is comparably straightforward because all that is required is the skill to evaluate a circumstance and adapt to it.

With the help of situational leadership, one can form a more relaxed atmosphere for employees because the style of leadership executed will generally fit their requirements.

This style of leadership takes into the many levels of growth in employees and aids in addressing the level of skill and needs of each employee.

6. What is the Role of Situation Leaders?

A leader executing a situational kind of leading will assess a team/group or organization and modify their course of leading to fulfil specific requirements of the organization or team/group. Situational leader enforces flexibility and adaptability into their leadership and daily evaluates the circumstances to ensure they are leading in the most relevant and successful way.

Typical characteristics that a situational leader demonstrates or is competent in demonstrating in the work environment include the following:

- **Direction:** There are organizations and teams that need a heightened direction level to be victorious. The role of a situational leader is useful in providing direction and delivering regular supervision.

- **Flexibility:** Because situational leaders regularly adjust their style of leadership to fit the present situation, it is required for them to show flexibility and be able to adapt on a frequent basis.

- **Promote Participation:** Situational leaders will constantly motivate their team fellows to be more self-sufficient by encouraging their engagement in decisions.

- **Delegation:** A thriving situational leader should be capable of delegating duties to all their team fellows who are capable of doing work unassisted. This is mainly right as the team of leaders gets more maturity under the guidance of the leader.

- **Frequent Coaching:** Situational leaders frequently ought to be competent to coach their group to promote growth and freedom.

- **Truthfulness:** It is required for situational leaders to be sincere about a circumstance and adapt their style of leadership to fit it instead of direct in a manner that is most beneficial to the leader.

A genuine situational leader is one who can victoriously evaluate their team and adapt different styles of leadership to fulfil the requirements of the team in each condition. In order to foster improved productivity and triumph across their teams, these leaders provide help where required and promote freedom and growth.

1.2 The Role of Flexibility and Adaptability in Leadership

Given the intrinsic stressors present in our society and economy, it is unquestionable that work environment instability is extensive. Transition is unavoidable. For exemplary leaders, it is easy to comprehend, and they can skillfully adjust to changing situations. Additionally, they are strong enough to face the unpredictable and difficult circumstances these changes can carry.

Let's dig deeper into this and examine the four causes why adaptability and flexibility are important in leadership.

1. What are the Key Distinctions Between Leadership Adaptability and Flexibility?

It is crucial to first understand the terms of adaptability and flexibility before examining why it is essential for success.

Adaptability and flexibility are usually utilized conversely, however there are few main distinctions among them. While the concept of adaptability is the capability to modify your situation in order to fit in a new atmosphere, the concept of flexibility is the readiness to accomplish. Your flexibility level is directly related to your willingness to alter and negotiate.

For instance, consider this scenario that your firm is going through some structural modifications that create a change in working hours; you need to work on the 3 to 11 pm shift now (which was previously the 9 to 5 pm shift) while embracing new squads, clients and needs mirrors your adaptability and how frequently you are keen on embracing this newer schedule displays your flexibility.

2. Why Good LeadWers need to Maintain Adaptability and Flexibility in Work Environment

These are the primary reasons why good leaders need to be adaptable and flexible:

To Grow Out of Difficulties

Leaders who are adaptable and flexible see the worth in obstacles instead of skipping the conflict. Rather, they handle the challenges with their head high because they know there is an opportunity to learn from mistakes and obstacles.

Analyses demonstrate that leaders who are not adaptable are represented by their coworkers and bosses in these manners:

- Risk evasive

- Not welcoming to new and various plans

- Defensive

- Not open to feedback

Because adaptability and flexibility promote new modes of thinking, leaders who possess them have the emotional mastery needed to:

- Grow out of mistakes and address them with stability

- Be open-minded and reply satisfactorily to the feedback

- Remain Organized when in pressure

To Make and Modify Plans

Being capable of establishing strategic and nicely organized plans is not the only element of good leadership. It also entails developing agile strategies that are adequately agile so that when unexpected challenges come your way, you understand how to handle them according to the situation. If you can accomplish, this boosts your worth and your team worth.

If leaders grasp various thinking and are willing to step out of their comfort zone, then they can easily adjust as the things around them change. Leaders who respond quickly are most likely to bring about change in comparison to those who are not open to adaptability and flexibility.

3. To Become More Equipped with Various Leadership Styles

A specialist in emotional intelligence, Daniel Goleman, describes that no specific style of leadership rules over another. Instead, the utilization of any style is based on the circumstances and people involved. Leaders should know and be keen on how to modify their style to match the special requirements of every new circumstance.

These are the six styles of leadership described by Goleman.

Here are the six leadership styles Goleman discusses:

- **The Coercive Style:** This implicates a "do as I tell" strategy reasonable for high-stress circumstances requiring a quick reply.

- **The Authoritative Style:** Leaders explain a prevalent plan to the members of the team and motivate them to accomplish it utilizing their unique methods, which is specifically helpful when trying fresh strategies.

- **The Affiliative Style:** Putting team members on top; this approach concentrates on promoting team unity and enthusiasm. Leaders must select this to assist members of the team to comprehend and use compassion in their daily dealings.

- **The Democratic Style:** In this style, members of the team have an equal say in making decisions and creativity. Leaders often pick this style to begin cooperation.

- **The Pacesetting Style:** Leaders form lofty expectations that they also display, usually utilized with team members who are highly driven.

- **The Coaching Style:** Mostly utilized for personal evolution instead of work-connected tasks, useful for team members looking to refine their flaws.

To Build Thriving Teams

In order to make their teams stronger, elements which eventually help leaders are the ability to learn from errors, strategically modify plans and include diverse leadership styles. Adaptability and flexibility are distributed to other team members when they are demonstrated on the leadership level.

All problems need a span of change, be it facing troubles or competing deadlines, and if the team members are willing to welcome these changes, they will become stronger.

4. What Does Professional Adaptability Appear Like?

Readiness to Learn and Grow

Adaptive leaders are consistently open-minded to learning. Failure never deterred them; rather, they accept failure as an element of learning.

A powerful leader may participate in these to improve their overall learning:

- Cooperate with other members of the team.

- Obtain feedback from coworkers and teammates.

- Ask inquiries.

- Start and take part in dialogues to evaluate how to readjust their approach.

Driven by Action

An adaptive leader is someone open to change and, in advance, discovers resolutions. They keep a powerful feel of urgency and concentrate on the task at hand to get it to fulfilment.

Carrying an approach driven by action may contain:

- Critical investigation of change endeavors in order to comprehend the task and the requirements for it to be finished.

- Creating milestones and smart objectives to ensure you achieve your goals.

- Developing meaningful metrics that fit with objectives to ensure initiatives remain on pace.

Resilience

Adaptive leaders have resiliency, and they also infuse this trait in others. Analysis reveals that resilient enterprises prosper when confronted with change and ambiguity.

Resilience can be embodied through these:

- Dealing with mistakes and drawbacks with calmness and elegance. Blunders occur, and the adaptable leader actively discovers methods to alleviate the concern.

- Using healthy dispute management. Dispute is unavoidable in the work environment among teammates. Adaptive leaders play a role in handling conflict that satisfies all sides when this occurs.

5. Ways in Which Leaders Can Enhance Their Adaptability and Flexibility

Leaders can enhance their adaptability and flexibility by utilizing these three fundamental ways:

Tailor the Approach of Your Leadership

To be a flexible leader implies operating with continuity. There is no single path to lead; the most suitable manner to lead people counts on different aspects.

- The members of the team you are directing.

- The capabilities, skills and readiness of those team members you are training.

- The situation's parameters, for example, project assignment and needs.

These elements evoke the kind of attitude you should display to effectively lead yourself and other teammates through the transition.

Some occurrences (like a project that needs to be done in a restricted timeline) might require an extra directive approach (like the coercive style of Goleman). Other circumstances (like supervising a teamwork training workshop with fresh hires) might necessitate an extra empowering or collaborative approach (this will correlate with the coaching of democratic styling of Goleman.

It is reliable for leaders to take some time to halt and reflect on the elements previously stated prior to answering their teammates. Leaders need to hover over each circumstance with the proper intent and mindset to generate the proper outcomes. The ability to prosperously steer through different circumstances can motivate leaders to employ and obtain a comprehensive group of leadership styles.

Achieve a Leadership Development Assessment (LDA)

You can also consider using LDA queries, which will help you figure out your present adaptability and flexibility level. Completing a 360-degree leadership development assessment can provide extensive insights into sectors where your leadership effectiveness can be improved.

Connect with a Mentor

The style of work is continuously changing and there are always people who are keen to convey the experiences of their leadership. Locate these professionals and acquire their information on essential lessons they have comprehended or a specific style of leadership that may be appropriate to your circumstances. A mentor is helpful for you in finding functional ways to use the correct style of leadership at the correct time.

1.3 Why Situational Leadership is Crucial

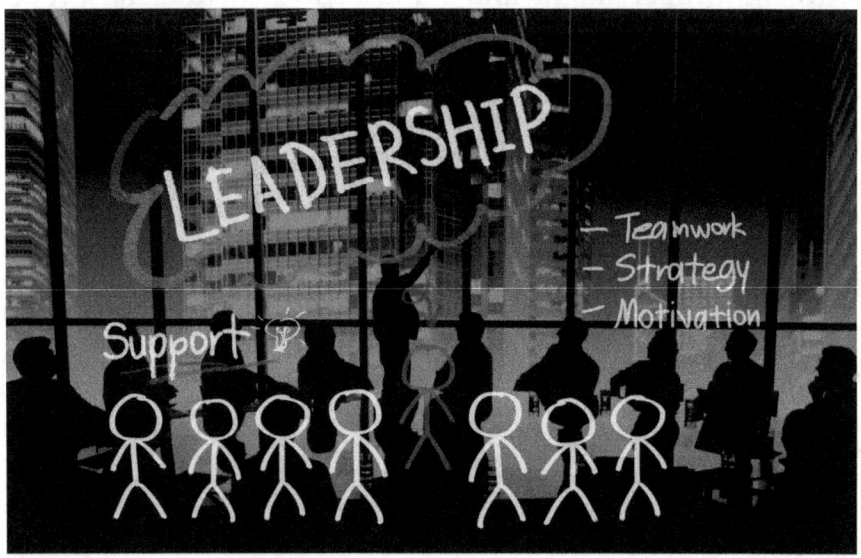

There are numerous reasons why situational leadership is crucial.

- Firstly, it recognizes the diversity and intricacy of the followers and the concerns that leaders encounter. You must be flexible to modify your style according to the particular needs and difficulties they confront.

- It encourages team empowerment and growth. By delivering the correct direction level and backing, leaders can assist their teams in developing and accomplishing their full capacity.

- Situational leadership improves a firm's effectiveness and performance.

When leaders know how to utilize the correct style for the circumstance, they can enhance quality, creation, productivity and spirit and lessen disputes and attrition.

1.4 The Significance of Situational Leadership Learning

In order to prevail as an excellent situational leader, you should learn the following traits. The best thing is that all these are easy-to-learn skills.

1. Flexibility

This is the main facet of situational leadership. It equips leaders to conquer obstacles, guarantee the success of their team and flourish in new circumstances.

2. Direction

Being clear about how to direct helps leaders to give practical guidance and aid to their teammates.

3. Delegation

This is an important skill for the leaders and their teammate's success. A situational leader should understand how to utilize their team's potency to finish the particular duties.

4. Coaching

This permits leaders to link with their teammates and assist them in reaching their maximum capacity.

5. Promoting Involvement

This skill is crucial because it is the duty of situational leaders to carry their whole team together and empower every teammate to be involved and thrive.

Learning these skills of situational leadership can empower you to create a successful, top-notch team that will remain relevant for a long time. Learning situational leadership is favorably advantageous for the firm because it creates a good working atmosphere and leads the firm toward success.

Chapter 2: Examining Four Main Leadership Styles

Let's dig into the core facets of leadership. The model of situational leadership, established by Hersey and Blanchard, is associated with offering the core examination of leadership styles.

The model of Hersey-Blanchard discusses the vital element of useful leadership development: the characteristics and styles of the devotees.

To become a great leader, one needs to understand that some people are on different compliance, maturity, motivational or intellectual levels. Various elements inspire various people, and this should be taken into consideration in order to become a tremendous leader.

Communication specialists highlight the significance of tailoring your message for your "planned audience." Because the objective is to inspire and impact followers and accomplishing this is only possible with a clear sense of the people you are attempting to inspire or impact.

Depending on the follower, the model of situational leadership discusses 4 kinds of leadership styles:

- Telling
- Selling
- Participating
- Delegating

2.1 Telling (Style 1)

Telling leadership style or style 1, is described by the leader employing medium to high quantities of Task Behavior and medium to lower quantities of Relationship Behavior. The telling style symbolizes the lowest leadership level. The majority of fresh employees need straightforward directions, so this is known as the "Directing" or "Telling" style.

The follower displays a lower competence level and increased commitment, stumbling to stick and encountering possible emotions of insecurity.

The leader should highly concentrate on tasks, instead of a connection with their employee, as a connection is not in existence yet.

Because of having less knowledge if the employee cannot do the assignment, the leader should come into action by spending more time to work with the employee, providing straightforward instructions and frequent monitoring. The leader needs to be motivating and inspiring, giving credit for the positive outcomes and rectification for less positive outcomes.

The purpose is to encourage the follower to upgrade to the next proficiency level.

This phase is significantly leader-driven.

2.2 Selling (Style 2)

Selling leadership style, or style 2, represents an approach of leadership which is high on Relationship and Task Behavior. Selling tackles followers who have gained some amount of competence and display increased commitment. The follower stays persuaded but is receptive to becoming collaborative and inspired.

The leader must concentrate favorably on tasks, and most of the leader's time is still required, but the emphasis now also includes establishing a connection with employees. Construct on the trust that was previously built and the motivation that has been displayed. The leader should dedicate additional time to hearing and providing guidance, planning further training for the followers if the circumstances need it.

The aim is to entice the follower to move forward to the next rank/level. There is a minor emphasis on "telling" and more emphasis on "suggesting," leading to greater encouragement and coaching. It is an acknowledgement of their advancement and inspires them to strive for more progress.

This phase is extremely leader-driven.

2.3 Participating (Style 3)

Participating leadership style, or Style 3, is essentially dissimilar from Style 1 and 2 because 1 and 2 are "leader driven", but Style 3 is "follower driven." Participating tackle follower who has achieved competence in the position but still displays rare inconsistency and has not reached maximum commitment. Regardless of being competence with their tasks, the follower might not be cooperative or doing as little task as possible.

The leader needs to engage with and back the follower. There are no longer requirements for a leader to give clear directions and follow up constantly, but are required to work continually with the follower to guarantee the work is being accomplished at the level needed.

The follower is currently strongly competent, but needs to be fully confident in their abilities and be completely dedicated to do their finest and thrive. The leader needs to now concentrate less on the appointed tasks and better on the connection among the follower, the group and the leader.

This phase is strongly follower-driven and connection-focused.

2.4 Delegating (Style 4)

Delegating leadership style or Style 4, is another approach of leadership which is "follower-driven," this approach is distinguished by low quantities of both Relationship and Task Behavior. Delegating is the greatest objective in which follower feels completely authorized and competent sufficiently to take charge and lead, with very little supervision. The follower is extremely competent, highly motivated, empowered and committed.

The leader can delegate assignments to the follower and supervise with very little follow-up, understanding that satisfactory or even outstanding outcomes will be accomplished. Both relationships and tasks need low concentration. There is absolutely no requirement to applaud the follower on each assignment, while it is good to give compliments for exceptional performance as suitable.

This phase is also extremely follower-driven.

2.5 Evaluating Your Default Leadership Style

We all face leadership duties at some time, regardless of our career route. Whether it is about taking charge of a short project or managing a whole department, there comes a point when we should direct a group of people in devising solutions to problems.

There are effective and ineffective leadership approaches, but there is not a single style which fits all. Leading a team can be accomplished through different strategies, and it is extremely vital to determine the style of leadership which matches your personality and the goals you wish to achieve.

1. Why it is Essential to Determine Your Own Leadership Style

Comprehending your style of leadership has a major significance for leaders. It allows you to estimate the impact of your leadership on those who are under your control and examine your own abilities and regions for improvement. While specific leaders can effortlessly recognize their style and its usefulness, many show characteristics from diverse leadership styles. Asking for feedback from everyone you direct enable a flexible approach, permitting you to integrate desirable features into your day-to-day leadership duties.

Transformational Leadership

Transformational leadership is a style that focuses on initiating transition and modification within a firm. Leaders practicing this approach strive to motivate their followers to reach their perceived abilities by unsealing their full potential. This style of leadership seems highly useful in firms that are undergoing crucial transformations and changes.

Key Features:

- **Future Emphasis:** Transformational leaders always look forward to evaluating the required actions to accomplish company objectives. They encourage their followers to embrace a thinking-ahead approach.

- **Focusing Change:** Transformational leaders are okay with change and understand the need for change for the success of the company. They work to make sure their followers are open and flexible to change.

- **Focusing individuals:** Transformational leaders recognize the potential of every follower and seek to establish individual powers and abilities to assist them in reaching their full potential.

Delegative Leadership

Additionally, known as "laissez-faire," delegative leadership concentrates on delegating duties to team members, embracing a hands-off policy. Leaders who pursue this style lean on their employees to accomplish their tasks without them being involved and micromanaging. Delegative leaders motivate their employees to employ their resources, originality, and knowledge to attain their objectives.

Prosperous enactment of this leadership strategy depends completely on the competence and commitment of team members. Regardless, it can also lead to conflicts among team members and possible division within the group.

Authoritative Leadership

Frequently referred to as visionary leadership, Authoritative leadership highlights a "follow me" strategy. Leaders making use of this style view themselves as mentors, which uplift and inspire those surrounding them. They give widespread direction, feedback, guidance, and encouragement to their teams, promoting a sense of achievement.

This hands-on style of leadership needs leaders to develop a personal connection with every team member in order to give guidance on a personalized level. However, leaders should sidewalk micromanagement tendencies that can be overwhelming for team members and can develop negative emotions.

Transactional Leadership

Additionally, known as managerial leadership, Transactional leadership counts on a reward-and-punishment approach. This style underlines structure, believing that people may lack inherent motivation to finish duties. In this style leaders create clear objectives and duties, determining the rewards or punishments for the work of their teams.

This leadership style of provide-and-take concentrates on efficiently adhering to designated practices and processes instead of creating transformative organizational modifications. Constant and congruent incentives with firm objectives are vital to avoid declining returns.

Participative Leadership

Additionally, known as democratic leaders, Participative leadership motivates leaders that employees should be involved in the process of decision-making. This style enables teamwork, accountability, and joint effort in issue-solving. The capability of sharing responsibility/power and effective communication are the fundamental aspects of participative leadership.

This historically dominant leadership style faces difficulties in current decentralized working atmospheres, like virtual or remote teams. Candid and open communications become important but can be tough to keep in virtual settings.

Servant Leadership

This style of leadership prioritizes placing the necessities of others first, which establishes strong connections and allows individuals to achieve their highest potential. Leaders embracing this style concentrate on comprehending and establishing the capabilities of anyone they work with, creating a positive example, and acknowledging personal objectives.

Servant leadership style highlights moral decision-making, cultivating an atmosphere where originality and issue-solving flourish. This process facilitates open communication, stopping conflicts, and constructing trust among teammates, eventually directing toward improved productivity and dedication.

2. How to Determine Your Style of Leadership?

Picking a style of leadership that best fits you can make you a more influential leader. Whether you organize a large team or a small team, your leadership style laboriously influences how your team witnesses you. Here are some pointers to assist you in getting started:

- **First,** being straightforward about your objectives and what you wish to accomplish is crucial. Having a clear vision makes it simple to convey your thoughts to your team and uplift them to pursue your lead.

- **Secondly,** be experimental. There are diverse leadership styles, and to find the best one for yourself is to experiment with different approaches and notice what suits you best and your team.

- **Lastly,** keep in mind that leadership does not imply being excellent but honestly leading. When you direct with purpose and enthusiasm, others will be inspired by you and your point of view.

Keep in consideration it is essential as a leader to be open-minded, ask for feedback, and be ready to modify your approach as required.

Chapter 3: Constructing Powerful Foundations

Leadership is a vital element of any thriving firm. For attaining success, a leader's capability to motivate, uplift and drive their teams is a common objective. Nevertheless, leadership is more than just about delegating duties and delivering orders. Influential leadership necessitates an extraordinary pair of skills and attributes that can be established with devotion and diligence. In this chapter, we will analyze the craft of effective leadership for constructing a strong basis for success.

3.1 Establish a Leadership Mindset

You may ultimately see yourself in a position of leadership, whether you handle a team of individuals for a corporation or run your own business. But failure and success as a leader totally depend upon how you establish a mindset of leadership.

There is a reason why people state that it's lonely to be at the top. Once you take a seat as a leader, you are encountered with making decisions that influence the lives of those around you. You may also be accountable for a whole organization. Doing this is never an effortless task. However, you will be responsible for all the decisions, so you have to establish the correct frame of mind to be influential in the position.

1. Essential Characteristics of Successful Leader

Find Ways to Success

Planning for success is an attribute of a good leader. In this manner, any steps taken can be resembled with the plan to ensure that they are aligned. When you showcase your thoughts, you can explain your choices by displaying how they donate to the overall vision or goal. This will simplify tackling any concerns or criticism about your choices.

Listening to others

Active listening is a vital characteristic of a great leader, which enables leaders to comprehend and manage the concerns of their teams. This enables a motivated and cooperative atmosphere where team members feel like they are being heard and are more likely to obey the leader.

Ready to Face Obstacles

Leadership applies to facing obstacles with a head high and seeing them as opportunities to learn and grow. The mindset of a leader implies welcoming hardships and stopping your team from getting burdened down by emphasizing positive results.

Decisiveness

The paramount of influential leadership is decisiveness. Leaders make fast decisions, voice them with confidence, and stay flexible when faced with transformation. This attribute guarantees that the team can steer challenges in a straightforward direction.

Humbleness

Humility is a fundamental trait of leadership, which allows leaders to confess what they are unaware of and value the contributions of their team. Accepting mistakes and sharing the praise and credit for wins' help establish trust and honesty among team members.

Accountability and Ownership

While successful leaders share praise for wins, they also bear accountability for any failures. They aspire to comprehend the causes behind failures, modify their approach, and guide the team toward conquering setbacks.

Ahead-Thinking

A leadership mindset is comprised of ahead-thinking, foreseeing future outcomes, and adopting change. Leaders who practice adaptability stop their firm from becoming unessential in a quickly changing market.

Empathy

Successful leaders display empathy, and they absolutely care for their team members' success. Knowing how to balance praise and productive feedback, providing opportunities for growth, and cultivating a unified team donates to the leadership's success.

Truthfulness

Transparency and honesty are the two main traits of leadership. Honest and open leaders construct trust, which leads to improved employee participation and productivity. Transparency in leadership promotes openness and donates to a positive work atmosphere.

Resourcefulness

Resourcefulness demands leaders to pursue information from various sources and stay open to different approaches. Effective leaders gain knowledge from industry leaders, but they also extend a wider net for motivation, which promotes innovation.

Leadership styles grow with time through error and trial. Effective leaders are dedicated to endless growth, altering and improving attributes that line up with their style and echo with their teams. The way to effective leadership includes a dedication to practice and master traits that donate to successful leadership.

3.2 Trust as the Foundation of Effective Leadership

Trust is extremely crucial in our lives. It builds the foundation of our connections, transactions and choices. Trust is not only just crucial in leadership, but it is also the basis of effective leadership.

Leadership is more than about personal glory. It is about empowering individuals. It is about establishing an atmosphere where individuals can attain their full potential, comprehending that their leader at heart has their finest interests. This is the point where trust becomes compulsory.

Leadership trust arrives from three primary elements: logic, authenticity, and empathy. These components are related and essential for constructing trust in a team or firm.

- Authenticity means being real to oneself. Leaders are trusted because of their consistency and transparency. If leaders are genuine, they become trustworthy and easy to approach.

- Logic in leadership comprises making the right and appropriate decisions and carrying out plans successfully. People have trust in leaders who display good judgment and profound knowledge of facts.

- Empathy in leadership is the ability to comprehend and care regarding the sentiments and needs of others. Trust is constructed when individuals think their leader actually cares for their well-being. Leaders who demonstrate an empathetic nature earn the loyalty and trust of their team.

In order to establish trust, it is essential to identify our trust wobble. This is the region where we may stumble in constructing trust associated with logic, authenticity, or empathy. Reminiscing on past circumstances can help determine our trust wobble and take measures to handle it.

Leadership begins with trusting our own selves first. In order to be empowering leaders, we are required to be sincere about our objectives, recognize our needs, and have full confidence in our thoughts and capabilities. Self-trust is the basis of constructing trust with others.

In successful leadership, trust acts as fuel for victory and success. Maintaining trust in our connections and with ourselves prepares the path for an effective leadership journey. Trust is important, and we can construct and keep it.

3.3 Role of Effective Communication in Leadership: Vital Skills and Strategies for Greater Productivity

Leaders have long acknowledged the importance of strong communication abilities, which encourage them to analyze different strategies for skill development. From avidly exploring the definition of leadership to registering in diploma courses to grow their communication abilities in order to be successful leaders, current leaders are taking diverse steps to overcome obstacles linked with inadequate communication skills in companies.

Let's start with comprehending the function of communication skills in useful leadership.

1. Why is Communication a Vital Craft for Effective Leadership?

Because leaders are a source of inspiration and empowerment for those around them, they should be brilliant in communication. Lacking powerful communication skills makes a leader's message go unheard and misapprehended. Effective communication is a crucial non-specialized skill that every leader must own. Here are numerous motives emphasizing the significance of good communication crafts in leadership:

Creating a Connection

Effective leadership counts on the ability of the team to finish the tasks consistently, and useful communication acts as an essential element in accomplishing this. Transparent communication of objectives, responsibilities, roles, and crucial information enables a powerful connection among the team, lessening disputes and miscommunications.

Constructing Trust

Trust works as a glue that ties the team together. Leaders who voice responsibilities and roles in advance clearly produce trust among the team members, encouraging a cooperative and trustful atmosphere.

Listening Actively

Leadership necessitates active listening. Leaders who understand when to hear and value the opinions of their team members earn trust and promote open communication.

Listening actively also assists leaders in comprehending their team in a better way.

Clarity

Effective communication maintains clarity of ideas, resulting in clear directions and dealings with team members. Clearly specified objectives and observing the progress assist in guaranteeing team success.

Capability of Asking Open-Minded Queries

Effective communication inspires teammates to ask open-ended queries, which fosters powerful bonds and assists leaders in comprehending their employee's inspirations and objectives.

Obtaining and Executing Feedback

Feedback is a helpful mechanism for self-improvement. In effective communication, leaders not only hear feedback but also execute it and give their team constructive feedback to improve continuously.

Body Language

Communication skills expand beyond verbal cues. Leaders should check on their body language to guarantee effective communication.

Effective Communication Role in Leadership

Effective communication and powerful leadership skills are connected. Leaders possessing useful communication skills can represent team objectives clearly, comprehend the aspirations of team members, and address resentments. Having effective communication skills promotes open communication, resulting in improved efficiency and productivity.

While it is true that not everybody is good at communicating, inspiring future leaders can improve their communication skills via different courses of leadership. These courses prepare people with the essential skills for successful leadership, enabling them to attain their career objectives.

3.4 Ways to Establish Leadership Credibility

Making credibility is important for building a high-performing firm and gaining the belief of your team. In the current transforming business atmosphere, credibility is a fundamental component in enabling cooperation, causing employee participation, and guaranteeing the victory of your firm.

Following are the useful strategies and tips to assist you in establishing a strong foundation of leadership credibility.

1. Display Genuineness and Integrity

Displaying genuineness and integrity is among the crucial elements of constructing credibility. Being honest about your values and always working on keeping them in your mind will assist you in earning the trust and respect of your team/group.

- Be evident and honest while communicating

- Accept when you do not understand something and be ready to learn

- Honor your duties and take responsibility for your mistakes

2. Grow Emotional Intelligence (EQ)

Emotional intelligence (EQ) is the capability to identify, comprehend, and handle your own sentiments and sentiments of others. Growing your EQ can assist you in constructing powerful relationships with your teammates and better steering difficult situations.

- Rehearse active listening and sympathize with others

- Handle your sentiments in high-pressure circumstances

- Give constructive feedback with respect and sensitiveness

3. Develop Expertise and Remain Informed

Your credibility as a leader is heavily impacted by your expertise and understanding of your field. By keeping yourself informed about trends in the industry and constantly constructing your skill set, you will be in charge of making appropriate choices and gaining the respect of your group/ team.

- Go and attend workshops, industry events and conferences

- Pursue options for professional growth

- Remain updated on industry news and the most useful practices

4. Be Receptive to Adaptability and Feedback

Remarkable leaders are consistently available for feedback and ready to adjust their approach when required. Being open-minded and showing flexibility in your style of leadership will convey to your team that you respect their feedback and are dedicated to development.

- Promote feedback and open communication from your team

- Be keen to review and modify your plans when required

- Learn by your errors and use those lessons when making future choices

5. Lead by Example and Empower Others

Lastly, to produce credibility as a leader, you should lead by example and encourage others to do similar. When you demonstrate the manners you like to witness in your team, you build a culture of high performance and accountability.

- Develop transparent expectations and hold yourself answerable for them

- Promote a culture of teamwork and cooperation

- Motivate innovation and inventive issue-solving

Keep in mind that credibility can't be constructed overnight; it needs effort, consistency, and time. But by remaining honest to your values, continuously comprehending, and guiding by example...

You are going to build a foundation that will put both you and your firm up for everlasting success.

Chapter 4: Navigating Difficulties and Resolving Conflicts in Leadership

Leaders can easily handle conflicts by actively hearing both sides, facilitating conversations, promoting empathy, recognizing common objectives, and fostering compromise. It's necessary to stay neutral and accurate when fixing conflicts. In this chapter, we will explore in-depth how to navigate difficulties in leadership and conflict management.

4.1 Common Challenges in Leadership and Suggestions to Overcome Them

Challenges in leadership are the obstacles that management members may face. These can possess issues with personnel or other external problems or internal factors that they need to tackle. Overcoming these barriers or hardships can result in a transformation in the staff, enhanced processes, and a stronger sense of belonging among team members.

1. Ordinary Leadership Challenges

Here are a few usual leadership challenges that leaders might often encounter within a firm.

Workplace Disputes

Disputes between employees or between managers and employees can disturb and interrupt the projects. Leaders are usually required to handle problems, facilitate conversations, and discover resolutions to sustain positive working connections.

Worker Distractions

Employees may encounter distractions in the work environment, which can affect efficiency and project deadlines. Leaders should encourage and back employees to lessen distractions and remain concentrated on their work.

Remote Work Issues

With the climb in working remotely, employees may face obstacles like technological problems. Leaders can lend support by guaranteeing access to essential instruments and keeping open communication to fix issues.

Layoffs and Job Transitions

Firms may go through layoffs or reorganization, making it challenging for leaders to effectively communicate, manage changes, and sustain team spirit during hard times.

Personal Obstacles

Leaders themselves encounter personal challenges, like lack of motivation or confidence. It is important for leaders to ask for assistance when required and keep a positive perspective, particularly when facing challenging circumstances.

Management Transition

Adjusting to persistent modifications in markets and business can be difficult. Leaders should quickly make choices, convey modifications to the team, and guarantee that everyone comprehends how duties may shift.

Team Growth

Growing and improving the skillfulness of team members is essential. Leaders can pinpoint places for progress, give new duties, and provide training options and resources to assist teams in evolving in their roles.

2. Tips to Overcoming Leadership Challenges

To reduce the problems of employees and handle the work environment challenges, leaders can consider doing the following:

Genuine Communication

Keep honest communication with the team about any modifications in the work atmosphere. Communicate any particulars about the business modifications that can affect the employees. Honest communication enables efficiency, boosts spirit, and displays faithfulness to keep the employees notified.

Listening

Motivate employees to express their concerns about duties, objectives and paths of career. Embrace a policy in which staff is allowed to comfortably express their problems. Address ordinary considerations in team discussions which promote an honest and open dialogue.

Practicing Flexibility

Be flexible with new staff as they adjust to their duties and steer workplace dynamics. Comprehend that remote staff may confront a learning curve and provide support as they adapt to new rituals. Address challenges and delays by having conversations about possible solutions like revised schedules and extended deadlines.

Being Compassionate

Display empathy when staff face individual challenges. Establish supportive agendas that accommodate their demands without generating considerable disturbance to the work atmosphere. Identify the distinctive challenges of office work and consider coming up with a more lenient policy.

Lead with Intent

Openly communicate the overarching aim of the firm and the action plan established. Include employees in the bigger company sight, which makes them feel valued and an important part of the firm. Motivate employees to share ideas and resolutions, promoting a sense of intent and participation.

Establishing Priorities

Openly explain priorities for your team in a dynamic work atmosphere. Give instructions on which projects should be prioritized, particularly when deadlines and timetables shift. Be open about expectations and distribute tasks as required to guarantee a concentrated and managed flow of work.

Offering Stability

Recognize the tensions workers may encounter, like job protection and financial problems. Offer stability by talking about improvement toward firm goals and handling any possible financial obstacles. While few shifts may be inevitable, sustain stability via constant meetings, praise of employee struggles, and celebration of landmarks within the work atmosphere.

4.2 Conflict Management Techniques in Leadership

A skill that assists leaders in building a successful team is conflict management, in which team members work jointly to achieve objectives, form strategies, and facilitate processes. There is a possibility of conflict when you form a team of people with different personalities, but understanding and knowledge of using conflict resolution skills can assist you in avoiding conflicts or fixing them rapidly when they happen.

1. How to Rehearse Conflict Management and Resolve Conflicts as a Leader

It is valuable to recognize what choices you own and when to rehearse conflict management. In order to solve conflicts smoothly when they occur, consider taking these steps:

Evaluate the Circumstance

It is important to determine the possible conflicts before they take place, as a leader. This involves assisting team members in comprehending processes or handling disputes among individuals. Evaluating the situation earlier enables you to create resolutions for conflict management gatherings.

Only Get Involved When Required

Not all disputes need quick involvement. Few disputes can be tackled by team members themselves, or they must be insignificant enough to disturb work. Get involved only when you feel conflict is not solved or when a conflict remains and needs your immediate involvement.

Make Guidelines

Making rules that promote a positive work atmosphere can assist in preventing possible conflicts. Prompting respectful manners and executing accountability for mistakes can demonstrate expected conduct, which reduces the possibilities of conflicts.

Understand Reasons for Conflict

Comprehending external elements that can affect confidence in the work setting can assist in controlling conflicts. For instance, modifications in firm processes may need extra support for employees adapting to the modifications. Pinpoint possible reasons that permit you to execute strategies like training events to minimize conflict.

Work Jointly with Conflicting Teammates

Cooperate with teammates involved in a dispute to discover a mutually acceptable resolution. Take the role of negotiator by promoting comprehension between disputing parties and working to find a solution that satisfies both parties involved.

Remain Neutral

Keep a neutral point of view to avoid giving the impression that you are favoring any particular side. Convey the message to disputing team members that you are not biased and concentrate on discovering a solution that satisfies everyone. Constructing trust is essential in solving disputes.

Staying Calm

Create a composed and professional environment during the meetings of conflict resolution. Your behavior sets the technique for discussion, and staying calm encourages a productive resolution process.

Concentrate on Facts

Facilitate team members to focus on the truths and reasons of conflict instead of sentiments. This technique helps unseal solutions depending on the correct information.

Keep Boundaries

Explain work setting boundaries to guide the behavior of your team members and avoid conflict. Maintaining these boundaries during dispute resolution guarantees mutual respect and comprehension of the conduct that led to the dispute.

Set Goals

Openly discuss the objectives of dispute resolution, like the wish for a productive and positive work atmosphere. Valuing one another's objectives helps in finding mutually useful solutions to the issues.

By taking these steps and implementing them in your work setting, you can practice conflict management.

4.3 How to Transform Obstacles into Opportunities

In both work and life, encountering challenges is unavoidable. These challenges give us a chance for self-growth and self-reflection because growth usually happens when strolling out of our comfort zone or attempting something unique. As a leader, the tension to sidestep challenges may be important, but adopting them is crucial for the success and development of the team. These 6 steps can assist leaders in steering challenges and transforming them into possibilities:

1. First Lead Yourself

It involves giving importance to activities that improve your well-being, like getting enough sleep, eating healthy meals, doing exercise, self-comprehension and emotional processing. Overlooking self-leadership can result in a lack of concentration, mistakes, and forgetfulness.

2. Take a Step Backward and Renew your Viewpoint

Regular stress of work can lead to losing view of the larger picture. Leaders are required to take a step backward in order to acquire a different viewpoint, guaranteeing they deliver clear guidance. Thinking forward and zooming out can lead to everlasting success.

3. Readjust with the Initial Plan or Upgrade the Plan

Once done with self-reflecting and earning perspective, leaders should assess if the initial plan stays viable. Obstacles may require adjustments, and leaders must be available to learn from incidents, build the team, and plan stronger.

4. Form Clear Attainable Milestones

A thorough plan consists of clearly stated milestones and little objectives that aid up to the overarching objective. Splitting objectives into little attainable parts stops stress and sustains team encouragement. Celebrating accomplishments at every milestone maintains momentum and inspiration.

5. Include your Team and Assist Them in Comprehending Milestones

Extraordinary leaders commit their teammates in the process of planning, confirming that they are on the panel, trust the plan and comprehend each phase. Outlining and simplifying the plan assists in maintaining the focus of the team. Dedicating some time frequently for your team to answer questions and get feedback enables a shared responsibility.

6. Estimate Your Progress Daily

Clarifying the plan and forming transparent milestones promotes easy progress assessment. Including progress analysis in the weekly ritual guarantees continued success. Determining divergences or absence of progress earlier permits timely adaptations.

Challenges are part of progress and can take various shapes, like emergency deadlines, customer demands, contending priorities, and handling virtual units. Leaders can utilize these six measures purposely in order to turn obstacles into opportunities for success and development.

Chapter 5: Boosting Employee Ability

The victory of a firm is closely connected to the performance of its workers. Involved and constructive workers play a key element in navigating a firm toward its objectives. Nonetheless, multiple leaders face complications in encouraging and improving their team's performance. As a leader, it is vital to purposely build work-setting structures and back systems that donate to the success of your team.

It this chapter, we will examine the importance of improving employee performance and give numerous strategies to maximize both production and satisfaction between team members.

5.1 Encouraging Empowerment with Situational Leadership

Enabling empowerment through situational leadership includes embracing a leadership approach that acknowledges the diverse requirements and capabilities of team members in various circumstances. Situational leadership is an adaptive and flexible leadership style that customizes the management methods according to particular circumstances. In terms of empowerment, this approach recognizes that people may need various levels of direction, support, or autonomy based on their skills, understanding, and the obstacles they encounter.

1. Ways to Empower Your Team Using Situational Leadership

Situational leadership can be a useful approach for empowering your team/group. But how to utilize it? These are some starter points on how to employ situational leadership in empowering your team:

- Firstly, evaluate every team member's growth level and accordingly alter your style of leadership. This implies identifying whether they require more independence or guidance in their job.

- Next, clearly and frequently communicate with your teammates. Ensure that they comprehend what you expect from them and give frequent feedback to motivate them even more.

- Be flexible in adjusting to altering circumstances or requirements among the team. Situational leaders should be capable of shifting quickly depending on various circumstances that appear.

- Promote open and genuine communication between the team members and encourage a culture of cooperation. By fostering teamwork, you can assist in building trust and enhance complete performance.

- Always display the manners you want from other teammates. When you demonstrate good leadership approaches; it motivates others to adopt the similar.

- By employing these techniques, situational leaders can constructively empower their teammates towards success while building a positive work atmosphere for everybody involved.

5.2 Promoting a Mindset of Growth

A mindset of growth is the faith that people can enhance their skills and abilities with feedback, effort, and knowledge. Cultivating a mindset of growth among your team is a vital element of constructive leadership. This approach highlights the idea that capabilities and brilliance can be established through hard work, devotion, and endless learning. By encouraging a mindset of growth, leaders encourage their teammates to accept challenges, keep going when they encounter drawbacks, and view struggle as a way to mastery.

These are fundamental techniques in promoting a mindset of growth:

1. Boosting Curiousness and Investigation

It is extremely important to encourage curiosity and investigation among your staff in order to imbue a mindset of growth and a culture of constant learning. This includes giving chances to employees to ask queries, experiment with fresh concepts and learn from their blunders. Providing resources, instruments and aid for seeking individual passions and interests can foster innate creativity, motivation, and invention.

2. Delivering Productive Feedback and Coaching

Another useful approach to promoting a mindset of growth is giving productive feedback and coaching. This implies giving timely, particular, and practical data on strengths, performance, and places for improvement. Helping workers develop realistic and demanding objectives, observing progress, and celebrating accomplishments donate to skill growth and developing confidence and resilience.

3. Encourage Cooperation and Peer Knowledge

Making a cooperative atmosphere constructed on belief and transparency promotes peer knowledge and leads to a culture of learning. Developing a culture where workers feel relaxed conveying insights, thoughts, and feedback to one another is important.

Encouraging informal and formal learning exercises, like coaching, mentoring, workshops, and online assemblies, enables the team to harness collective knowledge and various experiences.

4. Shaping and Gratifying Learning Behaviors

Leaders perform a major role in facilitating a learning attitude by shaping a dedication to improvement and development. Displaying a personal devotion to understanding and acknowledging employees for their struggles and donations strengthens the significance of learning within the firm.

5. Building an Adaptable and Supportive Atmosphere

Setting a flexible and supportive atmosphere includes giving workers the required time, resources, and space to learn and grow. Boosting them to make choices, take chances and explore ingenious solutions promotes adaptability when faced with challenges and the power to grab opportunities.

6. Assessing and Enhancing Learning Methods

Ongoing improvement of learning methods is necessary for maintaining a mindset of growth. Gathering and examining data on the effect of learning endeavors, and asking for feedback from customers, workers, and stakeholders, helps determine strengths, deficiencies, and regions for improvement in the whole learning plan, structure, and delivery.

By following these techniques, leaders can foster a mindset of growth in their team members.

5.3 How to Provide Constructive Feedback to Your Employees as a Leader

Constructive feedback is a vital instrument for leaders looking to promote development and growth among their teams. By giving on-time, particular, and practical feedback, you can assist your teammates in determining areas where they need improvement, attain their full capacity, and enhance their performance.

Here are some points that can help leaders give constructive feedback:

- Be clear – Clearly communicate the conduct or performance problem, employing detailed examples to demonstrate your points.

- Concentrate on the problem, not on the individual– Discuss the conduct or performance instead of creating personal criticisms or conclusions.

- Equalize negative and positive feedback – Underline both abilities and regions of improvement, supporting positive conduct and encouraging your teammates to thrive.

- Be on time – Give feedback as shortly as possible after an incident when the points are still new and appropriate.

- Facilitate dialogue – Ask your teammates to share their viewpoints and discuss possible solutions, enabling a cooperative and supportive atmosphere.

By learning the skill of constructive feedback, you can encourage a culture of ongoing growth and improvement, ensuring the success of your company and supporting the professional and personal development of your team.

Chapter 6: Lead with Assurance and Confidence

This last chapter concentrates on the basic elements of effective leadership, overcoming self-doubt and building confidence and resilience. Uncover practical insights to grow steady confidence and defeat self-doubt in leadership. Furthermore, explore the skill of resilience, learning the capability to steer challenges with adaptability and strength. This chapter presents practical direction on developing a style of leadership marked by resilience and confidence, important qualities for driving teams/groups toward victory and success.

6.1 Ways to Develop Leadership Confidence and Overcome Self-Doubt

Self-doubt can be a primary obstacle on the road to attaining confidence and success, particularly for leaders. It is realistic to feel insecure and nervous sometimes, but letting those self-doubts take a toll on us can stop and hold us from acquiring our complete potential.

Nevertheless, there are measures we can take to overcome self-doubt and construct confidence in our leadership capabilities. Here are a few of them:

1. Eliminate the Feeling that You Are Not Capable Enough

This thought is a major origin of self-doubt for most individuals. To defeat this, try reconceptualizing your opinions and remind yourself that every individual makes errors and it is okay not to be perfect. Concentrate on your powers and what you can give; do not indulge yourself in comparison with others.

2. Be Keen to Discover Something Unique

Discovering new things can assist in boosting your confidence and provide you with a feeling of achievement. So do not be scared to try new things and take a risk if it means going out of your comfort place.

3. Do not Strive for Perfection; Look for Goodness

Striving for perfection can lead to self-doubt, so ignore the notion of perfection and concentrate on performing as good as you can. Keep in mind that sometimes doing "good" is more than enough.

4. Employ the "Rule of Three" to Take the Best Decisions

When encountered with a tough decision, attempt to make a list of 3 options and consider the advantages and disadvantages of each option. This can assist you in making confident and knowledgeable decisions.

5. Take Adverse Feedback Courteously

It is realistic to feel angry when encountering adverse feedback, but attempt to listen to it with an open mind and evaluate whether there is any fact in it. Utilize it as the possibility to gain knowledge and grow instead of letting it break your confidence.

6. Failure Does Not Imply That You Should Not Believe in Yourself

Facing failures is a usual element of the growth and learning process. Do not let it shatter your confidence. Utilize it as a chance to contemplate and gain knowledge and then go forward with revitalized willpower and confidence.

7. Quit Harshly Judging Yourself

We all are our own most harmful critics but try to practice self-compassion and kindness and know yourself. Concentrate on your accomplishments and progress, and try to get out of negatively judging yourself.

Overcoming self-doubt is a continuous process, and it is realistic to have moments of hesitation or worry, but it is what you practice in those times that actually matters.

The best leaders do not let self-doubt consume their best self; they learn to walk ahead with full confidence in their leadership capabilities and themselves.

6.2 Mastering The Art of Resilience in Leadership

Only some individuals comprehend what leadership is. Not merely because they haven't witnessed and experienced it, but the reality is they need a real and valid picture of the leadership. The majority of the time, they believe, yeah, I am in the seat where individuals have to obey them, so they are the true leaders. They twist the seat with leading.

If a rank is granted, it can consequently be removed. A rank has a cost tag. So the one who gives the highest bid gets it. Any rank is temporary. Any change in the business and firm can take it away.

Let's look into leadership now. Leadership has an optimistic impact. A true leader does not desire the help of rank; he can impact others depending on what they have in them. Leadership is inside a person. It is everlasting. It accompanies a person everywhere. The influence of a leader can pervade into generations. Leaders begin by leading their selves initially. Therefore, personal leadership is the beginning of any effective influence. A nearer look at leaders will expose some very unusual characteristics. We will explain a few of these here; leaders exhibit what we call the elasticity principle.

Leaders have a remarkable ability to rise again from the challenges and experiences. Each one of them has a story. The determination of leaders is so praiseworthy that even in the most difficult moments, they sustain a positive mindset and attitude. They have a firm faith in accomplishing something more significant than them. At the same time, leaders who are dependent on their ranks can only stay for a short time. They quit their job at the smallest tension. They are unable to understand that leadership does not lie in rank. A rank does not make a leader, but it is the leader who makes a rank.

So next time you desire to take a role of leadership, keep in mind leadership is not about sitting in a carpeted room of an office and enjoying the luxury of being a leader. Rather, it is about spending the highest price and handling the tough tensions and hardships, solving issues, and caring about your employees.

To construct the craft of tenacity that leaders hold with them, you will have to make a choice to gather and make a team of people with the same character. You are also required to develop a feeling of self-awareness, which is understanding when to halt and ask for assistance. When we know our boundaries, and we strive to ask for guidance, we will be shocked at how much individuals were just here to assist us. Leaders have learned this secret. It is astonishing how we suffer in solitary, yet many individuals obtain great satisfaction in assisting others, particularly when they actively strive for support.

Mastering the craft of resilience in leadership is not regarding the significance of a tag but the persistent determination to grow out of hardships. Real leaders, navigated by a feeling of personal leadership, show resilience and an optimistic attitude even in the hardest times. Keep in mind that leadership is a voyage of self-awareness, comprehending when to pursue help, and recognizing the power discovered in cooperative support. By acquiring resilience and adopting the regulation that leadership is a constant process, you pave the path for lasting influence.

Conclusion

As you arrive at the final page of "Mastering Situational Leadership: Lead with Confidence and Maximize Employee Potential," I expand my honest thankfulness for commencing on this journey of leadership with me. Using my own knowledge and expertise, this book was written to provide you with the mechanisms to steer the intricacies of leadership. I believe it has supplied useful viewpoints on situational leadership, authorizing you to lead your team with full confidence and unlock their full potential. Thank you so much for your dedication to growing as a leader and for taking the time to read this book to the last. May your leadership path be loaded with never-ending success and positive influence.